The Blue Lonnen

by Katrina Porteous

Jardine Press Ltd
2007

The poems and photographs in *The Blue Lonnen* are selected from an exhibition commissioned by Alnwick Playhouse Trust in 2006 through the financial support of the Northumberland Coast AONB Partnership, which includes funding from Northumberland County Council, LEADER+ Programme and the Countryside Agency.

In addition to these organisations, Katrina Porteous, Nigel Shuttleworth and James Dodds would like to thank all the fishermen and boat builders, and their families, whose kind help and advice made the work in this book possible.

ISBN 978-0-9552035-5-8

Contents

List of Illustrations

Photographs by Nigel Shuttleworth
Paintings by James Dodds

Introduction

Katrina Porteous's sequence of poems in The Blue Lonnen is set, as her life is, on the spare and beautiful, long-limbed coast of Northumberland, facing the North Sea. Lonnen is the Northumbrian word for a lane, and the Blue Lonnen is a path, paved with the crushed mussel shells from long ago bait, which leads down through the fishermen's huts to the sea. At the end of it, until very recently, lay a boat, a coble, built and shaped for that shore and those seas, but which has now, after a long and honourable existence, been abandoned and removed, taken away in the end to decorate some distant caravan park. That abandonment is the subject of the sequence, a long and connected elegy, songs sung at the death of something precious, once treasured, now gone.

But the title has another meaning too: the blue lonnen is the way of the fishermen themselves, the blue path which finds its way through the alien world of the sea, both the broken surface and the unseen floor, using as its guide and for its marks the inheritance of generations, stretching back a thousand years to the Viking invasions, and doubtless beyond that.

In these poems, the two blue lonnens, that beautiful net of inherited understanding and the path with its abandoned coble, play against each other, marry each other and diverge: one, still, in Katrina's hands dazzlingly alive with energy and love; the other fading, forgotten, ashore, once the embodiment of the seaways, now a thing of sadness and even shame.

The collusion and coexistence of these two elements is what makes these poems beautiful. Like all elegies, they draw their life both from the life they record and from its ending. The poignancy and the heartbreak are inseparable from the beauty with which the old and disappearing things are seen and heard by the poet. It is of necessity an intensely concrete, physical engagement. There is nothing soft or mushy here; instead, something as felt and heard as the crunch of teeth into a green apple. It is the world of precise curves and the carefully located thing, beauty emerging from discipline not its absence. The hard-drawn sea and the dune-backed beaches are as fine here as the bones of a cormorant's skull. And she dispels the idea, so often maintained, that people who live and work in such circumstances are indifferent to beauty. That is not true because beauty itself – fully seen for what it is – is a guarantee of goodness. The bonny boat is a boat that sails.

Of course elegy is not enough. We can all feel the frisson of this wonderful language still being alive while the things and the habits and the knowledge to which the words were addressed, and by which they were formed, are shrinking and failing beneath them. These poems are in that way a set of tide lines, the pieces left stranded by the ebb. But still, after all, something good has been lost and that good thing is the human landscape of the fished-in sea, a world of hidden banks and reefs, the unseen rock lifting the swells into steepening surf, a knowledge in the fishermen, which exists only in their minds, never written or drawn, of the sea-bed realities beneath them. Those connected realities are forms of memory and transmitted knowledge, as if understanding itself were a crab-creeve, sounding in the inshore waters off this coast with no other instrument but the mind.

No new cobles are being built in Northumberland. The old ones are routinely destroyed, and where each coble required a whole community to crew and maintain it, the fibreglass work-boats which have replaced them are often manned by single individuals.

It is the loss of that connection and that shared inheritance which these poems lament, an elegy for a world, and more than that for a form of relationship with the world, which is disappearing as Katrina watches. Clenched nails rust, strakes spring apart and the beautiful figure-of-eight of the hull – a phrase and a visual understanding of the essence of a boat which Katrina shares with Nigel Shuttleworth, the photographer, and with James Dodds, the painter – loses the taut perfection first given it by the fairing eye of its builder. His only guide had been what looked right, shaping the timbers to a pre-imagined form. That is what has gone and that is a loss which is unalterably sad.

Adam Nicolson

The Blue Lonnen

The crunch of mussel shells under the boot heel;
The bramble-patch where the cottages were rooted;

The stone ring of the mussel bed, the stair
To the drying-green, the ballast heap, the beach of creeve-stones;

The tarry stain where the bark pot reeked; the wicket
In the wall; on the bridge to the limpets, the blade-worn groove;

The iron pin that marks the sea-road to the haven;
The nail driven into the door jamb – they are illegible

Without the rudder and the anchor,
Without the twine, the needle and the knitter:

For these are the paths they beat to the shore – The Nick. The Blue Lonnen –
And each is a road with a boat at the end of it.

How the Coble Came to Be

The sea made it. First
Its cold, salt draw-knife
Scoured the sky

Over Ross Sands and Fenham
Till it was clean,
A pure edge. Then

It carved out dunes –
Curves, as if land
Were like it. The wind

Whipped up a storm:
Two-thousand wings,
One heart, beating.

Next, it twisted
An auger through Budle:
The scream of a curlew.

Then out of the blue
Eye of the North Sea, its roll,
Its corkscrew swell,

Out of its craggy vowels –
Skeer, Carr, Steel –
Its guts between rocks –

From the precise curve
Of the cormorant's dive,
The sheer of its beak,

The hunter's lean line;
Out of the cuddy duck's
Broad beam, buoyant –

From this exact
Collusion of opposites –
From the sea that joined

And the sea that separates –
Onto the miles of sand
The first boat landed.

The Bonny Boat

Has she got a good high heed, your boat?
Is she laid-in right?
Does she look weel? Or does she coower hor heed, hor starn
Cocked up aheight?

An' has she got a right dip gripe, yon boat?
Does she draa' plenty watter?
Them modern boats, the heeds just blaa's awa'.
The forefoot winna haa'd hor.

So ha' ye got two masts aboard your boat
An' your lang tiller?
An' is your pitch-pine ruther dip withaa'
That ye can sail hor?

An' ha' ye got a right peak on your sail?
Your mast raked back?
Nowth-country boats could dae hor, lad.
One tack

For' Beadlin up t' Amble. O, a bonny boat
Will aye gan weel.
There's varnigh not a bonny boat been built
That winna sail.

Building the Boat

First comes the dance of nails.
Oak crook and larch –
Ram-plank and stem-post, scarphed,

And the planks slowly flowering outwards
From nothing
But the idea of rightness.

Like water, the grain
Flows and the plank bends:
Nothing forced or steamed.

From their grown shape
Arches the strength of each timber,
Each supple plank.

The boat-builder's measured eye
Judges. He is listening.
Composer of silence,

He does not make this tune,
But follows the line
To its natural conclusion

With draw-knife, chisel, hammer,
Smoothed by countless palms,
Father, son; with names –

Inwaver. Sewin'-nail. Drowt –
Planed by a thousand voices,
Shaping a dark procession.

The new boat waits.
Shored up with blocks,
Amphibian legs, it stands

Balanced on the brink
Of memory and future,
Poised, ready to move

From thought to wood to water.

Cathy

'See yon hyeuk?' says Cathy.
'Yon's ma life.'
Three-quarters of an inch of steel,

Barbed at the hyeutter, bent,
It glitters
Like a jewel.

Tiny. Cathy, six stone, volatile as petrol,
Wiry, lean,
Puts on her shawl.

Pleased to see you, kettle on,
Deaf as a sharpening stone
To every sound

Except the wireless static crackle
From the boat,
A little whirlwind,

She pegs the sheets out in the back yard,
Scrubs the step, stirs the pan,
Swabs the floor –

'When fetther hord it was
Another girl
He slammed the door.

Aye, but
He couldn't dae wi'oot dowters, ye kna.'

Cathy, bent
Beneath the creel:
Home from the mussel beds, the limpet pool;

Six stone of haddocks haa'ked aroond Reed Raa',
Husband, in-laws, tugging at her, kin
Needing her care,

Mussels to skeyn,
The boat to launch, lines to bait, claes to poss,
Sons to bear;

Cathy, bent with pains,
Years; busy as a sanderling,
Never still,

Down the harbour with the barrow, eyes
Blue as the Coquet, bright
As steel,

As hard, as sharp, as necessary
As a fish-hook
To the house, the men;

Cathy, without whom
A coble could not go to sea – as vital to it
As diesel, or the wind.

Boulmer Tractors

These Boulmer tractors – Zetor, Fordson Major –
Strong as lions, rusted, scabbed and holed,

Their four-square iron shoulders hunched, are waiting
Here, on the winter beach, at the edge of the world

Where the reefs lie horizontal to the shore –
The North Reins, the South Reins, Marmouth Scars –

A ruled line. A wall. This is the end,
This village with no shop, no bus. The wind

Scours down the road where every door is shut,
As if everyone here had grown too old, worn out

From staring east, from watching for the men
To steam into sight like spring with their boxes of salmon.

The next stop is a Conservation Zone –
Tractors, trailers, tidied away. Gone

Over to nature, if anyone knew what that meant.
The tractors wait for a movement order. Then,

Though their exhausts are blown, their tyres bald,
Like the great-grandmothers of men, in ragged shawls,

Straining every muscle, two abreast,
Heaving the coble up the beach, stern first,

Stoic, relentless, inch by inch – they will
Judder to life and, roaring, smoking, wheels

Flinging up rotten weed, salt spray and stones,
Rise from the sea, and haul the last boat home.

28

Family

Tonight, within sound of the sea, a man, no longer young,
Is getting ready for bed. Before dawn
He will slip out between black piers, alone.

He has three hundred creeves to haul: too many.
The diesel that Fastworker burns, no other way
To make a living but by hammering the sea.

It's not what he would choose. Nearby, the old boat
Loosens, slowly, nail by nail, opening out.
He is both sorry and not sorry to see her go.

There are few people left in the village who understand this:
She is more than a boat. She is a window
Back to where he came from. She is family.

Before he sleeps, he takes a breath. Tomorrow
Is forecast fair, there's not much wind. Along the row
A blackbird calls; and others echo, echo.

No One Said a Word

Off Howdiemont, the sea grows pale.
The sky turns silver-pink. The pools

Brim with light. The oystercatcher
Yelps, the turnstones rise, and over

The North Bay, the red sun flares.
It floods the holes, the Iron Skeers,
The bents, the Bathing House, the wares,

Without a sound. At the Weir Buses,
At Hip's Heugh on the Hinds' Hooses,

Not a single boat. No yellow figure
Squints, beatified, his fingers

Coiling the wet tow, lacing the creeves.
No wake of white gulls ploughs the sea.

No boot-sole prints the soft mud track
To Sugar Sands; and down the rocks

No woman bends her shadowy
Four-footed shape at Shallowarry.

The seas break on the Big Skeer,
Slowly roll over, a distant roar,

A taste of iron. A knotted hawser
Twists, a frozen current of water.

Split like an oak-stump, ten feet tall,
Riveted with barnacles,

The great pipe-organ boiler towers.
The seas around it blossom, flower,

Over and over. No one mourns
The countless quiet men and women

Who softly shuffled from this shore,
Their limpet creels, their swulls, their gear,

Their heavy hearts. No, no one heard
Them leave. Nobody said a word.

Plenty Lang a Winter

Howway doon the harbour.
Gan off afore the dawn –
Plenty lang a winter
T' lay abed aa' morn.

Plenty lang a winter,
Naen salmon i' the bay,
An' lang eneugh asleep, lad,
When your livin's rived away;

When your livin's rived away, lad,
An' the big man greeds your keep.
Plenty lang a winter.
Lang eneugh asleep.

Alnmouth

Something unassuagable about an estuary.
Black ooze, oily,

Clinging. Dragging east,
Miles of cloud rubble.

Acres of sea-purslane.
Redshank, dunlin,

Camouflaged. Dissemblance.
Chains of footprints

Snaking through mud. Loops
Of old rope. A curlew

Letting go its rinsed notes.
Abandonment.

And, slowly filling with water,
A boat

Rotten beyond rescue, its anchor-chain
Stiff; paint, lichen,

Flaking from its timbers, revealing
Strong, clear lines. What matters

Is sunk, uncovered
And sunk. On the far bank, a train,

A straight line on the heugh,
Hauling its troubles south.

And between them, the river
Slipping from green fields, Scots pines, gables –

Pink, blue, terracotta –
From the gull-squabble,

Towards something sparer:

Wormcasts.
Ripples.

On the far side of the water,

Walls, roofless.
Gleaming bent grass.

Its surface wind-hatched, stippled with light,
The river

Is letting go
At the end of its life, an old man

Catching sight of what matters –
That muffled roar,

The stern white line of the breakers.

The Old Boat

The old boat stands on the bank-top.
Long stains of rust
Run from her scut-irons, beadings. Daylight
Gleams through her rents.

Grass grows around her. Sparrows
Forage in the dry weed.
'A little worm has getten in ablow the scowbels,'
Billy said

Last winter. So they towed her onto the bank
And left her there
Like an old woman who has lost her reason,
Staring

Blankly at the sea, while the paint peels back:
The grain appears
In swirls and eddies, as if slowly
Returning to the tree;

Though still the straight planks fan
In their lovely curve, the flow
And figure-eight she makes – the geometry of beauty
Last to go.

They were hoping for a miracle.
That, half a century
After the first-clenched nail, Hector would fettle her.
But the years were too many.

This winter, nobody speaks of her.
No one can bear
To smash her up. To burn her. She is the sewing-nail
That holds them there.

She is the last link of the chain
That stretches away to sea, to the horizon.
She is the ruled line.
The end of the line.

Without her
There is no reason.

Sea, Sky, Stars

Cold tonight. No moon. The frost
Crackles on limestone. I'm staring east

From Beadnell Point beneath a sky
So starry, it steals my breath away;

North, to the Plough, and near the horizon,
Saturn, Sirius, Orion.

I'm trying to name them: the Byre-End Hard,
The Benty Smooth and the Barnyards –

The constellations of known ground.
Hills, hollows, rocks, sand.

Knot by knot, they wove that net,
Charlie, Billy, Ree'ford, bent

Each to the next men's ground, the next,
To Craster Smooth, Boulmer Sooth Hard,

To Cars'well Skeers, and south. Their marks,
Their grid of bearings, like the stars –

Not just a map, but a mesh of stories –
Lit up where and what we are.

Silence. The ebb's hush. What sails on
In us the sea will take, and soon

The dark, the stars. The grains of sand
Are not more numerous. This land,

The fields, the continents, pegged out
Across the surface of the planet,

Less dense, less populous than this
Black sea, starry and fathomless.

Glossary

Ablow – below

Bark pot – an outdoor pot used to boil tannin-rich 'bark' or 'cutch' to preserve ropes and nets
Beadings – wooden strips protecting the overlapping joints of planks in a clinker-built boat
Beadlin – Beadnell
Bent – tied on
Bents – bent grass
Buses – seaweed-covered rocks, e.g. the Weir Buses near Boulmer Steel

Carr – a rock
Cars'well – Cresswell
Claes – clothes
Coower – to cower, or droop the head
Creeve – a crab or lobster pot
Creeve-stones – stones used as weights in creeves
Crook – one of the timbers which fan out forward in a coble
Cuddy duck – eider duck

Dip – deep
Dowters – daughters
Draw-knife – a blade with a handle at each end for removing large amounts of timber

Drowt – one of the twin 'keels' on which a coble rests. See Scowbel

Fastworker – modern fibreglass inshore fishing boat built for speed, with large engine and planing hull
Forefoot – curved 'keel' under the bow of a coble, extending half way aft

Gripe – narrowing of a coble at the forefoot, to grip the sea
Gut – a path or opening, e.g. between rocks

Haa'k – to sell from door to door
Hawser – a cable
Heugh – a rocky outcrop, e.g. Hip's Heugh, Howick
Hind – an agricultural labourer. The Hinds' Hooses (houses) are a landmark at Howick
Hyeuk – a hook
Hyeutter – the barbed end of the hook

Inwaver – inner supporting stringer in a coble, on which 'thofts' (seats) rest

Laid-in – description of tumblehome or inward curve of a coble's top planks
Lines – long lines, which carried up to 1,400 hooks
Lonnen – path, lane

Marks – landmarks, lined up to take bearings

Poss – to beat clothes in water with a stick to wash them

Ram-plank – the bottom plank of a coble; in building, the first to be laid down
Reed Raa' – Red Row, a village near Amble
Rents – cracks which open up as a wooden boat dries out
Rive – to tear
Ruther – rudder

Scarph – to join wood to form a continuous piece
Scowbels – the twin 'keels' on which a coble rests, also called 'drowts'
Scut-iron – protective iron band at edge of 'scut' at the top of a coble's stern
Sewin'-nail – copper nail fastened with 'rove' (rivet), used to 'sew' planking together
Skeer – outlying rock
Skeyn – to shell, as mussels and limpets for bait
Steel – rocky promontory, as in Boulmer Steel
Stem-post – the outermost, upright timber running the length of a coble's bow
Swull – shallow basket used to hold long lines

T-netting – fishing for salmon and sea-trout using a T-shaped net anchored close to shore
Tow – rope

Varnigh – nearly, almost

Wares – seaweed
Wicket – small gate

A Note on Proper Names

'Cathy' is the late Cathy Armstrong of Amble. In 'Sea, Sky, Stars', 'Charlie, Billy, Ree'ford' refers to the late Charlie Douglas of Beadnell, Bill Smailes of Craster and Redford Armstrong of Amble, three representatives of a generation of fishermen born in 1920 or earlier. In 'The Old Boat', 'Hector' refers to Hector Handyside, the esteemed coble-builder of J. and J. Harrisons' boatyard, Amble. To all of them, with gratitude and the deepest respect, these poems are dedicated.